# AUTOBIOGRAPHY
# OF
# RAY-RAY

## & Other Ancient Ideas
## Like Hip-Hop

SUMMER HILL SEVEN

authorHOUSE®

AuthorHouse™
1663 Liberty Drive
Bloomington, IN 47403
www.authorhouse.com
Phone: 833-262-8899

Published by AuthorHouse 03/10/2022

ISBN: 978-1-6655-5282-0 (sc)
ISBN: 978-1-6655-5281-3 (e)

Print information available on the last page.

The front cover photograph is of the poet as a toddler
with his Mother – Jimmie Rebecca Simpson Lucas and
his Daddy – Bernard Robert Van Hoesen.
Photo Credit: Unknown.

Rear cover is based on a drawing from T. Elliot Mansa. Featured
rear cover photograph is of the author by Katie Clark.

This book is printed on acid-free paper.

Raymond Akbar, LLC
3236 Nekoma Ln * Tallahassee, FL 32304

# PRAISE FOR THE AUTHOR

Summer Hill Seven is a marvel and his journey is admired, indeed.

> ~ Adrian Hall, award-winning
> actor, director and playwright

Your Poemedy and recitation were cosmic! Thanks for sharing them with us.

> ~ Danielle Hillanbrand, University
> of Delaware student

Poemedy is a method of recording, analyzing, and codifying the Diasporan mirror. It is the quintessential pith of pain, rancor, joy and triumph of the spirit over those slings and arrows, the barbs and chains of post enslavement colonialism. In spite of the rigor of such analysis there is the good humor of grandma and the pungent perspective of the modern man all rolled into Poemedy.

> ~ Laurence Holder, award-winning
> director and playwright

This Summer Hill is more like a spring breeze, a fresh artistic air that has wafted on to the scene. For our continued good health we can only hope he brews up more salubrious weather.

~ Steve Tague, award-winning actor and director

My holy righteous humble seeker brother Summer Hill Seven is inspiring, uplifting, engaging, thought provoking and never ever satisfied with the status quo! He believes, as I do, that sometimes to make the world right side up, you've got to turn it upside down.

~ Dr. Laz, 2010 Teacher of the Year Award of Merit, National Science Foundation

Most artists talk about what they're doing and how unique they are. Then I see Summer Hill Seven with his Poemedy, mixing Shakespeare with civil rights, and then turning around to act in a play or make a movie. Summer Hill Seven has the walk to go with the talk, but he's such a modest guy that he won't tell you genius is smeared all over the pages of his books!

~ Aaron Joy, record label owner

I loved Summer Hill Seven's shows in Miami, I saw them both at the Byron Carlyle and the Adrienne Arsht Center for Performing Arts in the Piano Slam. Bravo!

~ Michelle Massanet, filmmaker

Summer Hill Seven's charm and wit carries over into his performances, writing, directing, and choreography – in every instance, he makes it look divine and effortless as he brings forth text that is inspiring, profound, and thought provoking.

~ Nana Afua, dancer/choreographer

Thanks for your creative and important work. I was so glad we could host you and hope that an opportunity arises for you to do more for Black American Studies in the future.

~ James M. Jones
Chair of Department of Black American
Studies University of Delaware

*Thank you to Anthony Zerbe*
*for reminding me to*
*never forget about Ray-Ray.*

"Never be afraid to sit a while and think."
A Raisin in the Sun by Lorraine Hansberry

# CONTENTS

## Chapter 3
### *Quiescent Reminiscing*

## Chapter 4
### *Of father & son*

# INTRODUCTION

Langston Hughes was my first poetry teacher. It is only now that I am deciding that I too am a poet. Until now acting was my only art. I have invented and written in the genre of *poemedy,* until now, to avoid being a poet. I only wanted to be an actor. As an actor I can portray any human of every variety. As a poet I am naked. My soul, my heart, my mind, my wit is laid bare before the world with no agenda or imaginary circumstances to hide behind.

As a poet I am also free. I choose freedom over the death that results from not making a choice. In my case I am now free from the desire to hide. We published our first book in 2004 openly hiding behind an invented identity. Here we share the story of a particular Ray-Ray knowing that there are and will continue to be many boys just like Ray-Ray who want to please their mothers. Ray-Ray finds very quickly that generally it is impossible to find complete satisfaction merely pleasing your mother.

Before, my mother, I wanted to please my grandmother. After my failed attempts at pleasing my mother followed regular failures at attempts to please teachers, peers, coaches, lovers, neighbors and other members of the community.

Poetry will not tolerate approval, acknowledgment nor interrogation. Poetry arrives unadorned, unarmed and unguarded emerging into an urgent empty reality.

May we meet in these lines and in between them as these symbols stand before the ultimate judge, bearing witness to themselves only. May the world be infinitesimally less empty.

The Publishers
April 4, 2022

xix

# CHAPTER 1

# Autobiography
of Ray-Ray

# Son to Mother

I am my own audience
Now that you are audience
In my head only. Mother.

I am still climbing.
Your inheritance left me
A crystal stairway leading
Upward. And I climb.

Up the first step of
Mahogany Obsidian
Climb onward onto
Carnelian steps, and up to
Tiger's Eye steps.

Still sometimes shocked
In the solar plexus of our
People's pain-body, Mother.

The crystals cut too.
Shiny sharp steps of
Rose Quartz and jagged
Turquoise steps as we wonder

Lapis Lazuli steps as we wander
Amethyst steps as we ponder.

I am my own audience
Now that you are audience
In my history. Africa.

America.
Gia.
Mothers.

You continue to climb, rise.
We continue to follow behind.
Dodging the invisible while
Seeking the indivisibility
That will ignite an audience
And excite our future to go.

Mothers you are gone or going
Going, going, gone.
Beyond merely a place
We go when we move on.

Mom you are not dead yet you are gone
America is not yet dead, yet she is crying
Climate change is provoking Mother Earth
To heal herself by detoxification.

We still climbing, in a climate sans control
Crystal stairs stepping from obsidian to amethyst
We followed you up from the basement
With bare steps up eight flights of chakras to the
Sun's light shining brighter upon the meek.

Mother wherever you allow us to go
We will go, we are your faithful sons.

Naturally inspiring genuinely gifted artist
Reflecting a quantum energetic remainder
Of all the sons under our sun. Afterall:

We realize we have everything
When you realize you are mourning
What you gave up to get everything.

# Bad Boy Blues!

10 years before the show hit the floor
I'm arrested at the exit of the bus door.

"Put your hands in the air."
Albany, PD doesn't bother with Miranda.

Today, cuffs in my new bell bottoms
And now around my pubescent wrists.

At 12 you know everything so
Surprise isn't wasted and fear
Isn't real for a real run away.

Learning the charge isn't
Running away
Instead it is burglary?

A glint in your eye reveals:

Your long sought credibility in
        the streets where heretofore
You're easy prey, has arrived, at last.

An innocent boy. A church boy. No more.
A charge without the crime feels more bad
        than the crime without the time.

Good, bad.

Being guilty of a burglary you
Didn't do - in our jungle - puts
More hop in your bop.

Now they know and everybody
Knows that you are really bad
In both the good way & the other way:
"Did you hear, Ray-Ray got arrested?"

Word travels at the speed of the streets.
Everybody looks differently.

Mom brings her fear of the white man
        hidden in her DNA, so she takes
        a plea deal, on my behalf.

No trial, obviously, since there is
No evidence, obviously, since I'm innocent
Of everything except my complexion.

A few shades lighter, I might of
Been safe, a few shades darker, I might of
Been dead.

But, I'm perfect. I have it
All and then some. I'm a good boy
Wearing the camouflage of a bad boy.

Bad boy, Bad boy - Ray-Ray
"You so, cray-cray."
So now whatcha gon' do?

# Hashtag Dream

It was ALL A DREAM! Hashtag dreams.
LA Law, except insert me in the scenes.

777 Figueroa was my first office.
FOI Malcolm on my wall,
Tupac in my Mazda RX7 cassette deck.

Tailored suits, cufflinks, silk ties.
Wearing the Mask that grins & lies.

Lawyering for Government entities,
Big Banks, and Mom's bragging rights.

Passing the hardest bar in America on the first try:
priceless. It only cost me my soul.

I had miscalculated the dream it would seem
      because I wanted to play a lawyer on TV, not in reality.

Who told?

The universe responded quickly
      by setting me free from my luxury
      cell in the sky.

Raymond Burr was my attorney
so, of course, he always wins.

Night became morning became night became endless
      regret that I was not living my dream
      of becoming an actor yet.

Cut to:

Me heading back to New York to find the dream behind the
dream.

The stage, rage, yet still another cage.
This time sans the land of sun
only tiny black boxes that became coffins.

Yes, this was my dream
      sleeping on couches,
      park benches,
      waiting tables,
      wearing the Mask
      that grins but discovers the truth.

It was ALL A DREAM.

SHAKESPEARE
AUGUST WILSON
SHERIDAN
SHAW
CHEKHOV
BRECHT
MILLER
PARKS
FUGARD
FULLER

The Atre
I'll always love you but Mom's in the sky
        and she was my only real WHY?

FATHERHOOD rescues me
        from early grave.

Begotten boy makes me reconsider how to behave.

IQRA!

That was the first act of this story
        and the author only knows how mine will end.

In the meantime and in-between time
I'll create mine. AUTHOR ME.

Today, I read a great play.
Played in my private paradise
        shared hope
        laughed
        loved
        and kept living.

Today my office is my garden
        my audience is virtual.

I auditioned in my kitchen
        and asked you:

What is your dream?
Because today I'm living mine.

## A Horseshoe Life

i live in the house
i finally bought for Mama
after she died.
On the mantle over
the fireplace
is the only picture
i own of her with my
father, Joseph, and me
it is my graduation
picture from high school
she is holding a pen
and a pad. That's
why I am a writer.
i don't have a picture
of her coming to my
college graduation
i gave a speech that
i wrote at both graduations
i gave the same speech
Twice in college because
the rain forced us to
have the graduation ceremony
Twice in the gym.

at both graduations
i was the salutatorian
Technically - i think
that says everything
about my life. i'll
never be a valedictorian
i think everyone
including me is afraid
to let themselves like
me. i didn't go to my
law school graduation
i gave the law degree
and bar admission certificate from
the state of california
to Mama as a consolation.

i'll never be a popular
writer like Langston
Hughes or James Baldwin or
Amiri Baraka instead
i'll almost be.
i'm an only child
with ten siblings and
none of them like
me and a few of
them love me but
i wonder about them
from afar - we are
separated by miles
words, worlds, wind
whispers and musings
we share a few memories
but nothing we can
build an institution

10

or even a phone call upon
i take all my words
worlds and musings to my
journal so the fact that
my son doesn't care
almost doesn't bother me.
i almost remember
mom wore a blue rose
and a purple violet
to the Tulip Festival
in Washington Park
on that Easter Sunday
the last time we went
to church together.

# Autobiography of Ray-Ray

The true story of a girl
who never had time to be a girl
so she never had time to grow up.

# mom I ate

Wait, eat something before you leave.
Your mother, if you had one, said it.
Eat something before you leave this house.
But Mom, they have food there.
It's a party. I can eat there.
What did I say? I don't want
No backtalk. She never defined
Backtalk. "I can't stand you."
The sounds storm out of the mouth in my mind.
Backtalk only got a backhand
When it came out of the mouth on my face.
Heavy-handed is the mother whose
Hands picked cotton in Alabama.
The tears formed in my eyes
though the hands didn't leave her side
or collide with my mouth, this time.
She was moved by the water to offer
An explanation - I could barely hear
Over the chewing of soggy canned peas
Drenched with snot & tears:
"I ain't gonna have them folks thinking I don't feed you."

# Ray-Ray Lives Alone In the Middle of the Ghetto

See, what had happened was
Cochise died because Mr. Mason
Intervened.

Ghetto life is unforgiving to both
Good Samaritan and charity recipients.
Jealousy, envy, black on black crime is
How we mark time in what used to be
The hood.

Ray-Ray lives alone
Ray-Ray prays alone five times a day
Ray-Ray eats alone one time a day
Ray-Ray makes love alone every other day.

Friendship is a luxury
Taxed very heavily in
Black ghettos. Those
Are the only ghettos Ray-Ray knows.

Preach couldn't trust Cochise
With his woman or ex-woman;
Ray-Ray knew before his ex-woman

Slept with his Cochise the outcome
So how come he pretended not to care
Even warned him in advance?
So he can laugh at them both.
He can laugh alone.

A ghetto townhouse in the south is like a
Penthouse in the north.
It damn sure beats death row
And solitary confinement
And the grave.

White friends are an oxymoron
Black friends are short lived
Jealousy, envy, black on black crime is
Remember, how we mark time.
It is not personal it is proximity
So if you are sensitive you
Probably want to find someplace
Else to live.

You can live longer in a ghetto
You ain't from because the grudges
Ain't that deep yet. The pain ain't
That personal yet. Don't forget to wear
Your "you ain't got shit clothes" everywhere.

White friends are an oxymoron
Black friends are short lived
Jealousy, envy, black on black crime is
Remember, how we mark time.

Ray-Ray has hung time, time and time again.
Now he lives alone in the middle of the ghetto
Happily ever after.

# That Nigga's Heaven On Earth

You will know your
Topia when you create it.
880, projects, desert,
beach, college, small, big
all adjectives to label
places created by other races & faces of
People. Ideal Cities.

I know you will know
Because I know I know
My topia - do you know
My topia - the Old Field. No?

Oh, well now let me see
Aha I see, I see...
Maybe you know a
different Tallahassee
Than me - but if you ever
been, you met at least one tree,
I knew it was the place for me
From the sound of the first word ever
Hurled at me from a speeding car down West Tennessee
Niggaaaaaaaaar!!!

My heart drummed louder
My head stood prouder
Mr. Nigger, my inner voice
Shouted!

If ever there was this
Mythical Creature, known
as a Nigga - I am him!

If you don't believe me
Ax my Niggas from
around the way.
Straight N I double g a
from since before back
in the day growing up
as little Ray-Ray
Even my momma
Could tell you about
that bad ass little
nigga Ray - Ray

So on this day
On West Tennessee in
My topia Tallahassee
I was again set free
by the confirmation

Why was the world
Even trying to be
denying me my full
respeck due as not
just a Nigga but

I am That NIGGA!
No matter of fact, I'm
That Motherfucking Nigga
You been warned.
You feeling some kind of
Way ain't you?

But look - this is mytopia
Carl Van Vechten had
His Nigger Heaven and
I have mine.

# *I'm 13 ½ and she's pregnant*

Shelly's cute little 15 year old face
With her short hair style
Standing under a south Albany bridge
Secretly sobs as she says the words.

That's all I remember.

I remember the amazing sex
    we had in hallways.
We had a lot of sex in a lot of halls.

On the living room couch outside her living room
    in the hall of her house on Clinton Avenue in Albany.

Amazing sex at the bottom of the stairs
    in the hallway of her aunt's house in Schenectady.

In the hallways of Albany High where we first met
    and had our first kiss.

I met Shelly in the hallway when I was 14 in the 9th grade
    technically, I'm 13 ½ and technically, she met me.

Peace, I'm that knowledge seed, Raseed
I've come to civilize the uncivilized, and set the 85
    free from mental slavery.

360 degrees of pure knowledge, wisdom & understanding.

We had a lot of sex in a lot of halls.
I understand. You want me to stand under you
    while we do this oochie coochie thing in the hallway.

That's peace.

# A Schenectady Self-Deprecating Gerund Rant

You big ol', looking-up every word - taking your time to read
the user agreement - thinking before you speak - getting
excited by obscure facts - glasses sliding down your face
fingers black with newspaper ink - no television havin'
reading 5 books at one time - more college degrees than
necessary - asking too many questions - talk to hear the sound
of your own voice - know everything about everything - met
everyone - officious, supercilious snob! Go the fuck back to
Albany, NY.

# sweet 16 with a nose opened wide by a white girl

Cocaine came and already knew my middle name
because Bernie was my Dad's name too.
Bernie did cocaine - not in front of me
but they were all doing coke back then.

Bernie was a gambler & pool hustler.
He never took me to work with him.

It was a *do what I say* rather than
A *do what I do* type of situation.

So before that night, I never saw cocaine.
After that night, it was years before I ever saw it again.
I knew how to drink and smoke herb
as well as anyone knows
How to drink and smoke herb.

I guess it lowered my inhibitions
which is funny because at 16, I couldn't
even conceive of spelling or using
a big word like inhibitions - I

Did not think I would go to college
I did not have a master plan.
The history is told in a somewhat linear
way by leaving out big chunks of
the story - like the night my older
sister - left me in the room with a $20
bag of cocaine alone & assumed

I knew what I was doing
I guess it was because I was from New York
upstate, but if you ain't never been
then to you New York means bright lights
tall buildings, and black boys that
sell and snort cocaine, apparently. I had

To my credit, had several sexual partners
I did not know cocaine was called 'girl'
I had only had sex with Black girls
I had thought about sex with
White girls but Black girls smelled
like home and nobody really likes
race mixing.

Cocaine is called white
girl too - so the irony of Black dudes
on the corner selling cocaine didn't
occur to me that first time
I snorted the whole bag
at my sweet 16th birthday party.

Happy Birthday to me, I guess.

# CHAPTER 2

## & Other Ancient Ideas Like Hip-Hop

*Love*

for god so loved the world
he gave to you, me
that is what she said
and i did not disagree
publicly

# Queen Blanca

Yes, I'm a white woman, true
    but you bet' not call my neck red.

Yes, I'm on welfare and
I'm Black by inception, too
    but you bet' not call me a wigga either.

My ancestors died so I can be
    on welfare, so kiss my wet unfettered
    white ass in the middle, two times.

# Silent Echo

Where does it come from?

It comes from the mouths of
    men and women long since silenced.

From the echoes of the sounds
From the mouths of men and
Women long since silenced

The men with the pens
Listened and painted
Marks only understood
By them for them
To remember the words
From the mouths of men
    and women long since silenced.

"Ain't no such thing as cain't"
Mama's first words that I remember
paying attention to

Mama's mouth has stood
silently echoing around the universe
for 15 cycles around the Sun.

"Ain't no such thing as cain't"
Where did she get
      that absurd idea from?

Echoes from the mouths
of the men and women
long since silenced:

"I have a dream that one day..."

Where did he get that absurd
      idea from?

Ain't I a woman?
All men are created equal.
If we must die, let it be like men.
What happens to a dream deferred
      does it dry up like a raisin in the sun?
Give me liberty or give me death.
E = MC squared.
Coke adds life.
Love conquers all.

Where did we get these
      absurd ideas from?

Echoes from the mouths
of the men and women
long since silenced.

Your words echo in silence.
What is unsaid is said more.

# The American Speaks of Winter

**(For Langston Hughes)**

I've known winter.
I've known winters from the 1900's
I've known winter in America
I've shared a joint with
The man who sang Winter in America
During a snowy winter night in the 1980's
Which for many of us was
A kind of discontented
Winter in America.

I've known the wet white
Winters in Arbor Hill, New York.
A wide white blanket over all of Albany
Even the Egg.

I've known the warm post-earthquake
Winters of Culver City, California
Broken homes and dreams
Scattered from Northridge to Santa Monica.

I've known the dazzling
Winter nights of Miami, Florida

From Brickell to South Beach
During Art Basel.

I've known icy Indianapolis, Indiana
Mornings driving past the Madam CJ Walker theater
Cold, slippery Cincinnati, Ohio winters sliding down
The hill into Walnut Avenue on the way to the Kresge center.

Walnut street was where Mama
Knew her final winter.

I've known frigid winters on park benches
On Central Park West and 5th Avenue, Washington Square Park
And on the Upper East Side, my thrice-driven bed of down.

I've known warm cozy winters
Around the fireplace in Queens Village, New York
With Shellie.
And freezing winters in
Times Square on New Years Eve
Rubbing noses with Billie.

I've known winters
Sitting here in Tallahassee
On a cool winter night remembering
Winter while beard grows whiter
Than the white winters I knew as a boy.

# The Ho' Blues

A pimp hates his bitches, ya hear?
Don't you know, a pimp hates his bitches
The only way to play the game
Is for a pimp to hate his bitches
While making love to them 1400 and 40 minutes
For three hundred and sixty five days each year.

# Divine Parity

I wrote a letter or whatever
    and I sent it via the government
    the other day.
I had no urgent message to deliver.

And it started off about bicycles and basketball
And drifted to my boys...

Back when I was a boy before
I declared and simultaneously willed
Myself into manhood at the Delaware Ave
boy's club in Albany.

I started this boy to man journey
At the Livingston Ave
    boy's club in the boxing ring in Albany.

What remains with me as memory:
Repeatedly running through Arbor Hill, NY
    my first neighborhood in Albany.

I won the fights in the ring.
And then, like now, I was alone.
So I ran all the way home.

I fought all my boyhood battles alone.
Sometimes, running, ducking and hiding
    see Sun Tzu, but not Bruce Lee
    was the art of war.

When I became Divine
    my battles were no longer only mine.

Many weapons
    foes
    enemies
    haters
    challengers
    have all been laid to waste.

Boys want bicycles and so did this now Divine boy
    he wanted a basketball
    eventually that led him
    to want exponentially more.

This boy wanted parity
    his pair of sneakers were *rejects*
They actually did cost $1.99
    they did make the boy's feet feel just fine.

The letter meandered...
From Dred Scott to Derek Chauvin.

The letter was all about being thankful.
Grateful to be an ex-boy smart enough to run in rejects.

I wrote a letter or whatever
    and I sent it via the government
    the other day.

I had nothing urgent to say.

In infinity
    saying is pointless.

In manhood
    saying is construction.

In boyhood
    saying is manifestation.

Smoking at a gas station is a metaphorical saying
That in infinity is beautiful
And in manhood is hazardous.

I wrote it and I licked the stamp
With my unvaccinated tongue.

Many weapons
    foes
    enemies

Virus is a word for an invisible enemy.

In the invisible divinity there exists parity.
There exists both divinity and *not divinity*.
Parity is anathema to *not divinity*.

A GOD to a non-believer
Is the very origin of their miserable protest identity.

Without ME
    nothing would exist for them to disbelieve.

Including and especially themselves.

I put the letter in the mail sans symbols on the envelope.
Men get lost in their symbols
    in their meaning making.

I wrote a letter and it didn't mean anything
    yet it is a thing.

I know because I did it.
That's what life gets to know.
Life knows it exists.

It does not require vaccination
    validation
    reparations
    bicycles or
    basketballs.

If YOU want it,
Parity also exists in divinity
    so divine discontentment
    is it's own taciturn medicine.

# That Was Easy

There is a thin line
Between Easy
And Lazy.
When I find it
You'll never notice.

# Indigenous Or May Flowers

you came over on the nina
the pinta & the santa maria.
maybe the mayflower.
we were why you came over.
vespucci who? never heard of him.

# Watching

Would what Jesus do
Be what Abraham Hicks might agree
God does?

He asks rhetorically.
She listens intensely.
He declares boldly.

I smile watching with no response
Outwardly or inwardly
Merely wondering. Marveling.

# Fruit tree blues

Birds, bees, flowers &
Caterpillars & poet
Trees with strange blue fruit.

# Soul still

autumn is summer's
raisin surviving in time
to see sun's decline

# Penny With A Hole In It

Think about not thinking.
Think about having no thoughts
What do you think; that's like
A hole with no penny around it.

I guess if I knew why she left me
She might still be here
Then where would I be
Sharing my days & nights with her?

A hole with no penny around it.
A lost soul that ain't never been founded?

In the solitude, the quiet stillness keeps me grounded
Reading is breathing in
Writing is exhaling
Living is an illusion
Dying is an opportunity
My love jones is simply
A whole lot of holes with no pennies around them.

# Something to Say (Gang-gang)

Enter stage left (audience right)
A poet. A silent poet.
A quiet poet. An American poet.
A neurotic poet. A plain poet.
A guru poet. A male poet.
A warrior poet. An actor poet.
A political poet? An experimental poet.
A spoken word poet? A comedic poet.
A skinny poet. A slightly overweight
Poet. A French poet. A Turkish poet.
A lady poet. A sufi poet. A hip-hop poet.
An activist poet. A black poet. An English
Poet. A Nuyorican poet. A teen poet.
An erotic poet. An Asian poet. A
Redneck poet. A philosopher poet.
A scholarly poet. An insane poet. An
Alcoholic poet. A funny poet. A
Rectum poet. A part-time poet. A
Girl poet. A food poet. A cinematic
Poet. A short poet. A long winded
Poet. A mobile phone poet.
An Iraqi poet. A gay poet.
A Christian poet. A gangster poet.
A nature poet. A charming poet. A

Sexy poet. An almost famous poet.
An actually famous poet. An
'I once was famous but not anymore' poet.
A female poet. A satanic poet. A secret poet.
A dancer poet. A reggae poet. An Ethiopian poet.
A blues poet. An Elizabethan poet. A Libyan poet.
An Egyptian poet. An Israeli poet. A Palestinian poet.
A Mexican poet. A Chinese poet. A Russian poet.
A Puerto Rican poet. A Lesbian poet. A xenophobic poet.
A homophobic poet. A highly judgmental poet.
A new poet. An old poet. An elderly poet. A senior poet.
A gray-haired poet. A college poet. A graveyard poet.
A science fiction poet. A wealthy poet. A broke poet.
An 'always complaining about not having money but happy to
spend yours' poet.
An adventurous poet. An intriguing poet. A captivating poet.
A Black nationalist poet. A white supremacist poet. A racist poet.
A progressive poet. A radical poet. A nigga poet. A honky poet.
An "I'm a poet & don't even know it' poet.

Finally they speak:

"What blight through yonder window breaks
T''is the east."
"Ay yo, anybody out here seen't
A poet up in this piece?"

# *Remember*

i aint forgot anything
i aint forgave anything
either.

you're going to have to
remember
to do that part on your own.

# She Smiles

She smiles and
then I breathe/easy
if her lip curls the
other direction, then I ache.

From the ache comes
art and from that
beauty follows.

She smiles and
the sun shines, rainbows
burst and kaleidoscope.

She smiles with
her soul, sanctified
saved, submerged.

She smiles so
art, beauty, soul
rainbows, kaleidoscopes
are saved.

# Her Winter Water

Winter Water works its way down
    my bedroom window.
The very same window - the only window
    in the room where we first made love
For the very first time
On the first night
After that first kiss.

Winter water waxes wondrously
About that first time.
Winter water wonders when
Will be the next time.
You will baptize me again.

Wading Wallowing Wanting
Waiting for your water
While you go away
Wet with possibility
Possibly wetter than ever
Possibly without you is the coldest
Winter whatever...

I don't want to think about
My reality without you
I'm staying here with
You in my imagination
While you spend the
Winter on the Water
While I wait here
    by my bedroom window
Wondering about the
Winter Water
Wait, what, I'm not waiting
I'm foreseeing a
Moment when we will
Curl up together and
Listen together and
Love together the
Wonderful Waxing of Winter Water.

# Heal Thy Tally Men, My Lord

Stare at a blank page until
You just cannot stand to stare
There any more but do it
Anyway - wait. Listen for
The 't' in listen then stare
Climb through the mounting mountains
Of marketing mottoes men
You will die before the top
Is complete so don't wait it
Broke the wagon pick a point
Dig in and around staring
At the sound you first found yet
Scratch, claw, forward in to cold
Fading warmth at your back side
Forget your preferred pronoun
Look upon thy tally men
With reverse dyslexia
Dig in your heals leaning not
On your own understanding
Of marketing mottoes men
Because they just don't mean shit
All the words you heard today
Were designed to sell some shit
Especially these sounds.

I'm here scratching & clawing
Hewing through it yet upon
A poem more poetic than poems
Skip the poems, pages omens
Scratch, beneath the mountain of
Sales slogans like heroes in
A prisoner of war camp who
Could, should, would and do leave
Every episode only to return
For redemption. The mountain
Is tangible, the threats are
Too dangerous for you to
Handle alone. Invent a God
And tell danger: Back the fuck up
My Lord don't play that shit, homey.
If danger ignores you, shank him.
Dig, scratch, forget how you lost
Your way. Shanking & Digging
Is the melody of your
Remedy to heal thy 3$^{rd}$
Eye: Self archeology
Is shawshank theology
Six humans murdered by cars
Let's blame the NRA, scratch
Must be getting my period
Very soon - ain't no sunshine
Inside the mountain - except
The sunshine inside of me
Without a release date
The mounting tension explodes
Dig, listen for the t in listen
Scratch, ignore the fluid dripping
Down my leg, rent-a-car, blame

The NRA, scratch, forget about light
Think about digging; claw with
Healing hands & Heels - Dig, scratch.
Take a lunch break.

# CHAPTER 3

## Quiescent Reminiscing

# Black Dog Cafe is a National Poetry Club

Money moaning is like
Monday morning on Sunday night.
By noon you have already moved
More toward the door of your expectation.

Birds fly high knowing that their
Presence is a present more receivable
At a distance since what the Seagull
Sells by Sally's shop on the seashore
Said simply, is a glimpse of it soaring.

Rays of Tallahassee sun shine on all 7 hills
Winter, Spring, Summer & then Autumn leaves
Fall from graceful indigenous pillars
Poetically called by the name with the sound
Parallel to the breeze for which they
Bear witness that the source is singular
Solo yet not solar so long as it shall shine.

Who wrote this - not who is taking the
Words down - down from a mind not mine.
Not surprised to learn. Learning implies

Surprise. Prizing to be present to the
*Newnicity* of all of it all the time - unless
It runs out on you like daddies do to moms.
Daddy don't dig departing yet the nest ain't
A thing that turns him off or on - he's gone.

Did or does Ms. Fitzgerald know about her
Body in Tallahassee near the road ready
To remember number 5? We know King James
Hooping and poetic names, yet what?
What about the two would be Emperors of the games
Not the same still both James will you
Still your mind & know @ Lake Ella off of Monroe?

Moving legs, lips, necks, hips while still
Sitting perfectly still. For real. FR
Is how that boy of mine says it - everything with
Almost no human noise whatsoever.
FR. FR? My response. Daddy won't let
That fly. Why? IDK. Wait, FR? Shrug
Human emojification renders me, myself
All this education, useless and /or/ pointless. FR.

# April. Fool!

The world cannot
Wait to kiss your ass.

You must have the courage
To show them your ass.

You must display the trust
To allow them to touch your ass.

You, finally, must spend time
To thank them for kissing your ass.

# Fatigué Blues

Working on the work
Makes us fatigué
Playing with the work
Reinvigorates the work
Leaves the worker exhausted.
Skinny. Straight.
Job knew something
Certainly before all
Was done and said he
Simply said: I'm done.

God was not.
Thus the fight for rest
And lest you forgot
God won that argument too.

I'm tired again and again.
Weary - I know I won't win.
But when I'm tired please let me rest, Lord.

# Journaling While Journeying

2/28/14 - 1:38 pm On a
Greyhound bus from Tallahassee
FL to Atlanta GA to
appear for one day (2/29/14 or)
March 1, 2014 as a background
actor in a Visa commercial
with Charles Barkley at a rate
of $200/day.

Like most of what I do
people often wonder what is
My motivation. The answer
is the story!

# *I'd March In Place*

I'd love you more;
Assiduously;
I'd talk less;
I'd smile more;
I'd listen more;
I'd laugh even more loudly;
I'd hold you longer;
I'd beg forgiveness;
Seven Ides and
Still zero progress.

# Last Kiss

What happens the day
You give your lover
The very last kiss ever?

Does she know there
Will be no more?
Do you know?

No.
There is no question
You never know.
Nor can you. No.

About the last
Kiss you give your
Lover - nor do you
Know the last
Kiss you will ever give
To your mother or any other
Make every kiss count.

Count every kiss in fractions
Demonstrate Love now. No?

What happens when you
Give your lover the last
Kiss ever?
How long can you still feel
It upon an open lip?

Since memory is fiction
How long can you fix
The last kiss in yours?

Do you remember your
First kiss from a girl
Other than your mother?

Yes, just like it's about
To unfold now.
        on 274 Livingston Avenue
        at a Birthday party for a
Kid, not me, and we 3
Play ever so joyfully - what is a kiss
To a 5 year old?

# A Lover's Poemedy

Have you seen her light shining
Embarrassing the daylight?
Have you heard her feet dancing?
Only everywhere I go.
Have you tasted her fragrance
With its promise of jasmine?
Yes, when alone in silence.

# A Risqué Poemedy

In your gaze I am new born
Cheerfully mewling, puking
Existing in your first touch
Thrusting, feigning and juking
Strangers always strange never
Sliding from noon to chirping
Birds dancing then repeating.

# Seven random twitter perfect poemedyz in random order

1. You are someone's fantasy.
2. New Year's days hope more follow.
3. Strong words will yield strong results.
4. In silence there's eloquence.
5. Every moment's the first.
6. Leap into the present now.
7. Hate is evidence of love.

# A Gram of Kisses

Count every kiss in fractions
5, 10, 15, 20 kisses
And then eventually the last.
Was it 21 or 42 or 84?
Did you lose count of the kisses?
Do you have your invoice?
Did you get all the kisses
That you bargained for?
Perhaps you are owed
Some kisses? Perhaps?
Count every kiss in fractions.
Perhaps that was your last kiss or not?
Maybe what interrupted your
Kissing may soon be forgot
Cuz baby...you just got this
Hot, savoir faire, amuse-bouche
Je ne sais quoi, kind of thing
Going on in your kisses & I
Been checking my paperwork
And I think you owe me one
More gram of kisses, mon amor.

# *Blue Note*

Blank page take me somewhere
I said, blank page take me somewhere
No where, where we have no air
Inside where we sit, and stare out into nowhere.

# Ism Defined

Is um, like you know, um
a thing, you know, like um, you know
is I'm making no sense because
if so then um, I am an ism
like as in

Romanticism where romance
reduces us to obedient rascals
running around currying favor
for the loss of love's labor /or/ even weirder
is eroticism.

Is I'm gonna have to break this down
to you too? Well, um, you know, Ero
is the hero of the ego, reducing us to running
around currying favor - chasing our tale, their tail
small tail and even whale tail often at the pace
of a jail snail /or/ more weird still
is afrotism.

Is I'm gonna have to break it down ABC style?
Afro as in Africa, rather than the hair style
Baptism, completely up under the water

Chisholm, as in Congress woman from Brooklyn
the first Black human to seek the US Presidency in Babylon.

Ain't nothing on earth as Afrotic, erotic & romantic
as a Black woman seeking the Presidency, like um
is I'm gonna have to break this down to you too
or do you remember Michele? Oh?

Well, hell, then the mother of civilization
has at last returned to sit on her throne
let us this moment cherish, as the Queen
of Clubs, trumps the Jack of Diamonds
and we inaugurate Vice-President Kamala Harris.

As we join hands in support for our, um, import
we become hand in glove, handling love
ero, afro, you know, um, ism.

# Chapter and Verse

If you can say, yes you can;
If you will be, your word;
If you will give your life;
If you can transcend gracefully;
If you believe unequivocally;
If you have been chosen
You are an Alpha man
Beyond Ice Cold
My brother, you are frozen eternally.

## Still

I am still
Being still who I am
Wrestling with what I am
Calling myself this or that
Only to take hold of who I am
As I pass from stillness into motion
Freeze, please so I can hold you
Hold us. Hold me. For one moment
I plead with you to remain an I am.

# Her Sonnet

Precious as you are mostly I ignore.
Not wanting to tax your energy, yet
Righteousness is not found in the east nor
Teachings from the poor west side's hamlet.
Yet here I am now begging you again
Undeserving talentless fraud I know
Competing against forces that will win
Submission is inevitable, so;
Together our victory will last
As sandcastles in the sky beyond blue
You driving and I make the shotgun blast
Destinations are new beginnings, true.
Sankofa birds both doing the tango
Spin, twirl side-by-side, above and below.

# CHAPTER 4

*Of father & son*

# Island (For Xalimon at age 13)

No Island is a man; yet
Hath a hungry mouth, that sings;
Pulsating percussive heart
Feelingly feeding foul ears
Preying devout eyes. Dark. Kind.
Ubiquitous Island Soul.
Still. Still inspiring purpose.

# Anointed Queen

When you are known for poetry
And then you come to know hers
When you are known for loving
And then you come to smell hers
When you are known for love words
And then you come to kiss hers
You crown her as an
    anointed queen.

# *Bolden*

Bold ideas are only
as good as
bold execution.

Bold execution is only
as good as eloquence &
a steady stream of bold ideas.

# You made me pray, prayer

I'm a sinner and I'm gonna sin again
I'm a sinner and I'm probably gonna sin again
But you already know Lord,
Because you made me & the devil didn't have shit to do with it.
Amen.

# You'll miss me first, Ms.

I'm in love with your body
I am afraid of your mind.

Don't you see, I'm in love with your body
    and scared to death of your mind.

Still, I will never let you go
    even when you leave me behind.

# Prehistoric Hip-Hop

Nigga's ain't afraid
of nothing but Negroes
because Negroes are
afraid of everything
especially niggas.

We traded the witch doctor for
which doctor, the rich doctor?
Yet the pain still remains.

Dreamers ain't afraid
of anybody except
Pragmatist because
They count success
In round figures.

Yet the pain still remains.

Never bought. Never bossed.
Makes you wonder how we
Keep from going under.
It's like a jungle most of
The time.

Yet the pain still remains.

# Drapetomania

A six syllable
word that means "crazy nigger"
swinging from a tree.

# South of the border of... Canada

I wander.
I wonder around.
I wonder if this is the sound.
The mumbling syncopated sounds.

The mouth of the new south.
Tallahassee are you the mouth?

I wonder.
I wander around. I wonder around
      anytown in the south, mumbling in my mouth
M - I - crooked letter, crooked letter
      mumbling around the new south.

Listening to murmuring from the south
      about mumbling from my mouth
T - Allah - as I see a synchronized south
M - I - crooked letter.

Belts on bibles and holes in shoes
      in my mouth, mumbling verses
      articulating blues echoes of an
Alabama, bama or Obama's mama.

All the friendly people are in church
　　　on Sunday in the south, so it's
　　　just us sinners wandering around Walmart.

Yo mama so south, so bama.
I wonder and wander around
　　　anytown around the south and wonder
　　　in which south
I AM!

# Project Windows

Forgive them if they stare
These pupils of the ghetto
Domiciled in a world where there is despair
Full of petty important shit
You have helped put something in it
So you have helped fill the unforgiving minute
With a few seconds of pretty distance run.

# Preaching to and for the Choir

God is Love
Love is God
Love is not Sex
Sex is not God
Therefore
What?
God does not
Approve of Sex
Therefore
I am a virgin
until the GODLY
Man comes along.
Somebody say
go on with
it, brother minister
YET WE KNOW
God gave <u>all</u>
of us 1
method to continue
God wants us to procreate to
Continue to
populate -
Repeat after me
brothers & sisters -

I must copulate
to procreate
and God wants me
to procreate so
we can continue
to populate his
Kingdom on Earth -
Somebody say - go head
Brother Minister - go head
tell the truth the
whole truth so help
you God Almighty

Therefore - here is what
God wants right now
Brothers & Sisters - right
now - he wants all the
Godly people to get together
and copulate - now you might
not just yet be ready to
Procreate - but he wants
you to start practicing -
Today - Let that virginity
Shit Go Amen - Don't be
a nun by default
Because you aint giving
nobody none - you have
become a nun by default,
Find a Godly Man -
and give him some
today

"But pastor, I cant
Find nobody -
All the Good men
is taken -"

You damn right
they are - that's
how you know
a Godly man be
cause - in these dark
days of Drapetomania
& *disquiescence* -
A Godly man
Has to be able
to handle more than
one woman.

- Somebody say Pastor
I didn't know you were
gonna tell the whole
truth TODAY! I
thought you were gonna
ease 'em into it.
No, no, no - we
cant ease it on 'em
we gotta stop war
Challenge greed
Combat nakedness How do we
do it - with LOVE
And love's chief is sex
Love sends sex to
do the dirty work!

Sex takes the wrap
when things go
off kilter

Sex gets the blame
for love's decisions

A man sees a
Woman's booty
and he elegantly reshapes
the word in his
Mouth - calls it
beauty - and sends
In Sex to his duty
to do the dirty work.

If you gonna do the
Dirty work
Do the Dirty work
With a Godly man
And if that man has a woman
Then you have a conversation
With that Godly woman
If necessary.

Because sometimes you
Got these squatters
They don't want the
Man they got and
They aint about to
let nobody else have
him neither.

Let the Godly man's
word be the last
word on the subject
- you are being courteous
by talking to the woman
- we have already
Established that
the man is the
head
- If you in rebellion
against that then
aint none of this
gonna work anyway
- But if you in rebellion against
that - you aint
gonna be in here
very long -
not in this congregation
- say Amen.

And If I am still
a virgin over the age
of 18 I am going to stop
being a nun by default.

I am going to copulate
today or at the latest, Tomorrow.
Now please pass around the collection plates.

# Never Never Love

I loved you once
You loved me twice
The 3rd time will be the charm
Let's forget about the future
And dance together tonight as if it's the past
Don't remember - forget me not
Yet let go of what we think
We know about each other
You know I'm selfish
And I only want you
All to myself all the time
I'm too selfish to tell you this
You might decide to be all mine
All the time - You might decide
I'm right all the time - You
might decide that love is not
Like Santa Claus or the Easter
Bunny or Unicorns
You might decide that love
Is like taxes, death,
Blackness in America or
Concrete buildings in
New York City. You might
Want to marry me and have

My babies and be perfect
Yet let go of what we think
We know about each other
You know I'm selfish - let go of that
And I only want you - let go of that
Let's dance together like it's the past
Let's dance together like we
Are the first two beings to
Ever dance to music
Let's pretend that love
Is real the way we pretend
Justice is real
Let's forget about the
Evidence - Let's tell the
Truth and lie to each other
So we can vertically lie
With each other. Just dance, hold
My hand and don't ever
let go of that.
Jamais
Jamais
Jamais
Amor

# Before Love

Before Same Sex marriages
Before the Internet
Before Brown beat the Board of Education
Before Habeas Corpus 1679
Before the 14th amendment was compromised
Before the 4th TV Channel
Existed - Before the 14th
Star was sown on to the red, white & blue flag - Before
Ft. Orange became Albany
Before before
Before 1619 brought human
Traffic - Before jumping
the broom - Before I loved
you. I loved you and I still do.

# Sufi Haiku

Am I self serving
Or am I serving you, God?
Alhamdulillah.

# Once in a while

mom wore a blue rose
quiescent reminiscing
of father & son

# Lust

Penetrate your soul
Entering every hole
Nature does the rest

# Endless Loop of Gratitude

I'm grateful for my mammy and pappies.
I'm grateful for all the sad, lonely days
And all the days I fell asleep with the happies.

The park benches, because the ground is hard.
Grateful for Walter Dallas.
And Jewel Walker who gave me an alarm clock
So I can be grateful that I graduated from the PTTP.

I am grateful for Sandy Robbins telling me that my Shakespearean
Monologue was the worst he had ever heard.
I am grateful for Leslie Reidel telling me to "do it exactly or don't
come back".
I am grateful for every soul ever caressed by the PTTP.

I am grateful for the opportunity to have played with the REP.
I am grateful for every single step on the journey of art.
I am grateful.

I am full of gratitude despite what anyone may think of my
attitude.
I am so grateful that I am changing my name to Grateful.
I am grateful to be grateful to be Grateful with you now.

# Inhale/Exhale or Equinox

Paper, scissors & rocks.
Bubble, bubble spoils of Trouble
We don't need!
No.
No more trouble.
Or souls on ice
After the soulstice - now long past.
Time still ain't money
Nor even time.
Once upon a story of LOVE
You're going to want to
Remember the burden of
September & School.
Of Hard Knocks.

More & Amor
And even Sommore
Queen of Comedy
For all Times.
Trenton makes and the
World takes Sommore
For all Times.

Times ain't paper or scissors.
Time is a pen filled with big bold
Beautiful bleeding rocks
Spreading more and more light
Both night light and daylight
In equal ways.
Yet no bearer of burdens
Shall bear the bare burden of the burdened.

More & Amor
And even Sommore
Spreading equal pay
For Kings & Queens of Comedy
For all Times. Enjoy life all the time.
Bear the bare burden of life, all the time.

#MeToo
Mooning you.
For all Times.
We don't need!
No.
No more trouble.

Equal pay, for equal work
Equal wages for equal pages
Equal banknotes for equal burdens
Whether the burden is with paper
Whether the work is with scissors
Whether the burden is with Comedy
Whether the work is with Poetry
Whether the burden is with Rocks
Or not with paper, scissors, Comedy, Poetry, Rocks
Equal PAPER for equal BURDEN.

Believe.
And now breathe.
Believe.
And now again breathe.
Let your heart & pen bleed
Sticks & stones
Breaking the bones of inequality & iniquity
Like rocks.
Rock.
Put your hands in the air and wave them from side-to-side like
you really do care.
Rock.
Rock

Paper, scissors & rocks.
Bubble, bubble spoils of Trouble
We don't need!
No.
No more trouble.
After this here
EQUINOX.

# About Poemedy

Eloquence is our business. Eloquence is fluent, persuasive speaking and writing. Summer Hill Seven is recognized as one of the foremost leaders in the conversation on creativity & eloquence in America.

He is a distinguished alumnus of Princeton University, New York University School of Law, University of Delaware's Professional Theatre Training Program, and Richard Stockton University.

Karen Hunter, the Pulitzer Prize-winning journalist and New York Times bestselling author has described Summer Hill Seven as "truly one of the most important voices of our time."

You may schedule a private lesson, class, workshop, lecture or performance with Summer Hill Seven. You may also purchase our signature eloquence products including books, cd's, films and quality apparel. Each of our services and products reflect our complete love of all that is eloquent. Our methods deliver unique results in the following areas:

- Acting Lessons
- Public Speaking Lessons
- Creative Writing Lessons
- Personal Appearances

- Consulting Services
- Creativity Therapy
- Private Coaching

To learn more about Poemedy's one-on-one coaching, text "SPEAK" for an appointment now, 213-537-5887, or visit www.poemedy.com.

## SUMMER HILL SEVEN

actor • attorney • author

*a sojourn starts with one step*

# SQUIRCULAR

*An Actor's Tale*

"Summer Hill Seven...is truly one of the most important voices of our time."

## Karen Hunter

New York Times bestselling author and
Pulitzer Prize-winning journalist

Summer Hill Seven once again is pushing the boundaries of political correctness. He is truly one of the most important voices of our time.

~ KAREN HUNTER, PUBLISHER, PROFESSOR, PULITZER PRIZE-WINNING JOURNALIST, & NEW YORK TIMES BESTSELLING AUTHOR OF STOP BEING NIGGARDLY.

Squircular! makes me imagine what Antwon Fisher's book might have been if he had combined his poetry and his memoir; both Fisher and Seven's stories are beautifully triumphant yet only one is poemedy. Honest. Passionate. Raw. Artful.

~ DAVID LAMB, ATTORNEY/ WRITER/PRODUCER

Brilliant!

~ LINDA RHINIER, NJ COLLEGE ADMINISTRATOR & FREQUENT ARTS PATRON

Get the f... out my head!

~ KWAMI K. KWAMI, D.A.D.

## PRAISE FOR SQUIRCULAR!

Squircular! pulls no punches. I love the seamless intersection of Seven's story with Palin, five percenters and the Nobel Peace Prize. These jump off the page for me as rich in uncommon insight and deeply introspective -- in the way that forces us all to look within and see past the grand pageantry of power and politics.

> ~ BRYONN BAIN, ARTIST/
> ATTORNEY/AUTHOR

Terrific! Cool!

> ~ SANFORD ROBBINS, ARTISTIC
> DIRECTOR OF THE REP/PTTP

Well done in capturing the Orwellian sense of our modern politics.

> ~ SALADIN M. AMBAR, PH. D. AND
> PROFESSOR OF POLITICAL SCIENCE

Brutally honest and moving. At moments a bit unsettling, but then redeeming.

> ~ ANONYMOUS

Squircular! is a unique, poetic and uncommonly keen account of the Black experience.

> ~ JAMES M. JONES, PH. D/CHAIR
> OF DEPARTMENT OF BLACK
> AMERICAN STUDIES AT THE
> UNIVERSITY OF DELAWARE

# HÃNG

A POETIC MEMOIR

# TIME!

SUMMER HILL SEVEN
AUTHOR OF "NOTES OF A NEUROTIC!"

INTRODUCTION BY LAURENCE HOLDER

# SUMMER HILL SEVEN

# NOTES OF A NEU- ROTICA

Poet Tree:
Essalogues,
Plays &
Poemedies

# Of Poets & Poetry

A PUBLICATION OF THE FLORIDA STATE POETS ASSOCIATION / VOL. 46.3

F
S
P
A
INC.

*See page 3*

summer hill seven

MAY 2019

Spring Fling

Photograph by Akil DuPont

www.FloridaStatePoetsAssociation.org

# Profiles in Poetry

## SUMMER HILL SEVEN:
## Actor, Author, Director, Educator...

*There is a very long string of nouns one would need to use to be fully informed as to the skills and identity of Summer Hill Seven, but one word might sum it up—accomplished. The following questions, composed by Al Rocheleau, and responses in Summer's own words, allow us to peek into his richly-textured life.*

**Q:** The Summer Hill Seven name is a memorable one. The story?

**A:** My great grandmother, whom I never met, raised my mother, who was orphaned by her parents. My great grandmother's name is Cora Summerhill and she is the seventh of 13 children fathered by Robert Summerhill. When my mother transitioned in 2004, I published my first book (Notes of a Neurotic) as Summer Hill Seven. When I completed my MFA in acting in 2007, I then chose Summer Hill Seven as my stage name. The idea is that when you see me (or read me), you see my mother, her mother and all the circumstances that lead to who and what I am.

**Q:** You've lived a long life, come a long way. What got you here?

**A:** I have come this far, by faith, as the gospel song says. Nothing else. By Faith, I am referring to the biblical definition—"the evidence of things unseen and the substance of things hoped for..."

**Q:** You're an attorney, an activist, an actor, a poet. How do those roles go together?

**A:** The common denominator is the persuasive use of language. From as long as I can remember, I chose to believe that the right word was the magic and often secret password to unlock the door to all of our desires.

**Q:** Is the actor a poet inside dramatic lines, the advocate a poet for his client and his cause?

**A:** That is a persuasive way to describe it, for sure; now that you put it like that, I will say, absolutely.

I never chose poetry as a path, poetry actually intimidates me in ways that few things have. Simon Callow, a British actor and writer said that the theatre benefits most from "actor-poets" which to me, meant actors who value above all the poetic possibilities of language. I relate to that and after I read that I began to explore it more deliberately in my own acting work. In fact, I intend my appearance at the Spring Fling to be my final public performance for my own poetry. I intend to confine my performance of poetry to film acting and the works of other poets. As far as, the advocate being a poet for his cause and client, in my first book, Notes of a Neurotic, I did include a letter that I wrote on behalf of a legal aid client prior to retiring from the practice of law because the rhythm of the words felt artful, if not poetic.

*(Continued on next page)*

*2006—Professional theater training program, University of Delaware, Summer Hill Seven protraying Sir Anthony Absolute in the play The Rivals by Richard Sheridan. Photography by Paul Cerro*

**Q:** Who were your personal life-models, beacons, famed and otherwise?

**A:** Naturally, my first super-hero was none other than Jesus Christ, the blue-eyed and blonde version, no less. After Jesus, I discovered the rock band–the Monkees, they were my first friends. I watched their tv show and sang and danced along with them. In puberty, I discovered what the idea of "Black-ness" meant for a young man in America. It is important to add that by birth via Robert Summerhill and my Gramma the beliefs and traditions of the indigenous people of this land we call America were passed along to me in direct ways. Chiefly, I always understood that I was in "the world" but not "of the world"–that the material world was temporal, and of little consequence. So, by the time I encountered the story and legend of Malcolm X, I recognized my story in his. I also recognized the story of Jesus of Nazareth in Malcolm X's story. I didn't choose him as a life-model rather I saw Malcolm X as a beacon, as you say, a guide that could help me through the valley. In college, when some fraternities began to approach me about joining their organiza-tion, that is when I chose my first and perhaps last life-model, Paul Robeson. Now, I don't see myself as anything more than a mere particle connected to all the other particles inside the ALL.

**Q:** Can you tell us about the Poemedy? One might assume the combination of "Comedy" and "Poetry," but would that discount it? Is it more like Dante's definition of Comedy, of our real Life Story?

**A:** Laurence Holder is one of America's greatest writers and I enjoyed the distinct privilege of learning directly from him for several years. He wrote the play that brought Denzel Washington to the attention of New York theatre critics when Washington played the role of Malcolm X in Holder's *When the Chickens Came Home to Roost*. I learned from him about the origin of the term Jazz. I had not yet written any books. I had started directing plays in New York City around the same time that I met Holder.

*Above: Image from a reading at Miami Dade College, 2009*

*Below: Photography by Paul Cerro*

At the same time, Danny Hoch and his cohorts were starting to develop what they were calling "hip-hop theatre"–it was very exciting for young pigmented actors because theatre is very racially segregated and so, many of us felt like this new form would bring greater opportunities for us, the hip-hop generation, to express themselves on stage.

At the same time, David Lamb was writing novels in a new literary form that they were calling "hip-hop literature" –eventually after refusing many offers of other writers to adapt his novel for the stage, David decided to adapt it and produce it himself. Hoch, Holder and Lamb and I come from a philoso-phy that Elijah Muhammad, the teacher of Malcolm X, called Do For Self.

David Lamb, happened to be my roommate at Princeton and NYU School of Law. Eventually, he and his wife chose me to adapt the play version of his novel, which he wrote, for the stage. It was the first play I directed. I had begun writing Notes of a Neurotic. I understood that we were way off the beaten path with our efforts and if it was successful, we may want to retrace our steps to figure out how we arrived at this destination, and what would we call this destination. This is years before In the Heights would blow the world away. This is before Spoken Word would come to Broadway. We were out on a ledge poised to jump into an abyss. David and his wife asked me to diect the play. It was one of the greatest gambles that I had ever taken as an adult. I had no idea what I was doing but I had absolute faith that it could be done and that we could do it together.

During that time, I wrote and directed my first film about Summer Hill Seven, a fictional Spoken Word artist. In the film, a mockumentary,

*(Continued on next page)*

Of Poets & Poetry

*...formane of Shakespeare N. Haarlem in Miami/Project
...-Hop—2010. Photography by Tony Mahammad.*

*...03—Poster for Shakespeare N. Haarlem stage play, NYC*

Summer Hill Seven is asked something like what would replace Hip-Hop after it is no longer popular and he responds: "Poemedy or would you prefer, cometry?"

After the film, the term Poemedy stuck with me and we began to listen for the distinction. Someone else, whom I have yet to know had written a book titled: Poemedy. For me, it allowed me to create without regard to fitting into externally imposed descriptions. Eventually, I started seeing poemedy everywhere...in George Carlin and Richard Pryor. When I learned about Dick Gregory, I immediately cast him as the Godfather of Poemedy. Yet, Amiri Baraka's work was where I first saw an opportunity for poetry as advocacy. I started bundling it all under Poemedy. Poemedy eventually became my reason for being. Since, money was never a motivator, the only reason I kept doing anything was because I felt like the world would benefit from Poemedy. My job was to persuade them that it would give them life more abundantly.

Q: Where did the seven-syllable structure of your poetic lines come from?

A: Do you remember when I mentioned that I discovered Blackness in puberty? Well by the time I was in middle school, I began to reject most of the academic curriculum as an affront to my blackness, preferring instead to learn on my own or from the words of black thinkers. It was the spirit of the times. I was always an honor student, which often meant I was the only or one of a few pigmented students in class. I started skipping class whenever anyone mentioned that we would study Shakespeare. White Jesus and Shakespeare were the chief tools of colonialism. Consequently, I was very ignorant, and in some ways, remain very ignorant of the western cannon.

So when I was given the opportunity to attend the University of Delaware's Professional Theatre Training Program (PTTP) - the only MFA program in America at the time dedicate to performing, almost exclusively, the works from the Western Canon, I jumped at the chance. Primarily, because I was working and creating in New York City but I was without steady income and a place to live. But also because I saw Denzel Washington play Richard III and Jeffrey Wright play Mark Anthony in Julius Caesar and I had faith that I could stand on any stage in the world and perform any material like my personal life model–Paul Robeson–who played Othello.

Shakespeare was the next big challenge and to get paid to fail at it was an offer I simply would not refuse. And fail I did. It was painful for a nearly 40 year old (and here I will use the term Black) man to humiliate himself daily in front of a bunch of white people. I was the worst student of Shakespeare, certainly in my class, maybe ever. Everyday I had to fight with myself and smoke a joint just to go back to class for more humiliation.

My classmates were either confused by my presence, or some were openly hostile to my presence. I think some of them felt that I was taking a spot that they knew other people would do anything to have, especially since the chance to study with the PTTP only came around once every four years.

Well, I had already published my first book and since I did not know how long I would be there before they asked me to leave, I started thinking about what I was going to do next. Again, I was given the privilege of performing at the Tony Award winning Utah Shakespearean festival because after a year of absolute humiliation I managed to create 90 seconds of Shakespearean acting in an audition monologue. Talk about going from the frying pan (of whiteness) into the fire of whiteness - if there is some place whiter than Cedar City, Utah then I don't want to know about it.

*(Continued on next page)*

Of Poets&Poetry 5

2009—Summer Hill Seven portraying Boye from Jesse B. Semple Suite, Jazz at Lincoln Center. Photography by Frank Stewart.

Image from a reading at Miami Dade College, 2009

I turned 40 years old that summer. For my own sanity, I decided to write a follow-up to Notes of a Neurotic, dedicated to "all the Black men in America who had not and would not reach the age of 40"–men like Dr. King, Malcolm X, Tupac, Biggie, Emmett Till, and too many to list. In this book I decided to organize them around these seven-syllable statements of my personal beliefs I call perfect poemedyz–the first of which is–Life is a game–play to win.

**Q:** You are deeply involved with the work of grandmaster poets of the African American experience such as Langston Hughes, for which you developed an entire show. Do you identify with or perceive you are carrying on the work of the Harlem Renaissance, or equally of poets such as Tolson, Baraka, or contemporaries like Patricia Smith?

**A:** I think of Langston Hughes as my poetry mentor. His sense of humor reads so beautifully to me. It is his poetry that I have performed more than the words of any one person including my own. I have never appeared in any of his plays. I have performed Boyd in his Jesse B. Semple stories with the Jazz at Lincoln Center Orchestra. He is so loved that when you say those magic words the world falls to your feet–it is intoxicating. In some ways, I think I both avoided poetry and attempted to emulate it with poemedy because of my envy for Langston Hughes' gift with words. If Langston was poetry, I did not imagine, nor did I believe, nor did I have faith that such purity, and beauty could come from me–but I could tell my story of isolation in a way someone coming after me might feel less alone. It is the telling of the story of isolation that connects me with the Harlem Renaissance. This period was when an intellectual elite came together and said let us make art on that great void that signals to all living and yet unborn that they are not alone.

**Q:** You are a champion of poetry education. What have you been doing in this regard, and what do you see happening with our young people?

**A:** This is what my documentary film, the Poemedy Project is about, what works in education. The film led to the Poemedy Institute, where we offer private lessons, classes, workshops and events. We have taught the art of Poemedy to Alvin Ailey summer camp, Miami-Dade Public Schools, Leon County Schools–used the techniques to help executives become more persuasive leaders of their organizations. This past election cycle, the Big Bend Poets & Writers began engaging Leon County civic leaders in a dialogue about pragmatic uses of poetic rhetoric. The mission of the Poemedy Institute is to change the world by changing the words of the world; and to teach creativity and eloquence as an alternative to violence.

**Q:** What do you want to accomplish with your work moving into the future?

**A:** I'll know it when I feel it. In this moment, I feel as if I have about a dozen film characters that I want to lend my voice to sharing, including Nate Love (also known as Deadwood Dick,) Othello, Lear, Malcolm X, Elijah Muhammad, Paul Robeson, Dick Gregory, Langston Hughes, Amiri Baraka, maybe even Summer Hill Seven ;-)

I want to publish all my writings into a single anthology.

I have more energy I want to give to the Poemedy Institute which is dedicated to teaching, investigating and advancing eloquence, especially as an alternative to violence. I hope a future generation will continue to believe what my first hero is quoted as saying: "these things and greater, shall you do..."

Links to videos of Summer we think you will enjoy: Link, Link,

Of Poets & Poetry

## April 15, 2004
*(Excerpt from Hang Time: A poetic memoir)*

What happens the day your mother dies?

"It ain't no Sunshine when she's gone
    And she's always gone too long."

I remember my fifth Christmas
Without you because some
Southern cracker locked you
And daddy up for driving while black.

Too young to be sad
Too naive to be mad
Seeing you eventually
Made me glad; cuz we
Celebrated when you came back.

After 35, 36, 37 and 38?
I needed you more with every
Rotation of the earth around the sun.

Yet seeing your face staring at me
    in the mirror
And hearing your audio track in my mind
Is warmer than the sun:

It's heart warming being your son
Not your first but your last son
Not your only
Not your special
Not your favorite
But your son
I remain your son.

"It ain't no Sunshine when she's gone
    And she's always gone too long."

© 2005 Summer Hill Seven

## Winter Water

Winter Water works its way down
    my bedroom window.
The very same window - the only window
    in the room where we first made love
For the very first time
On the first night
After that first kiss.

Winter Water waxes wondrously
About that first time.
Winter Water wonders when
Will be the next time.
You will baptize me again.

Wading Wallowing Wanting
Waiting for your Water
While you go away
Wet with possibility
Possibly wetter than ever
Possibly without you is the coldest
Winter whatever...

I don't want to think about
My reality without you
I'm staying here with
You in my imagination
While you spend the
Winter on the Water
While I wait here
    by my bedroom window
Wondering about the
Winter Water
Wait, what, I'm not waiting
I'm foreseeing a
Moment when we will
Curl up together and
Listen together and
Love together the
Wonderful Waxing of Winter Water.

© 2019 Summer Hill Seven

# About the Author

Summer Hill Seven was born in Albany, NY in 1965 and given the name Raymond Bernard Larkins. He would change his name many times. He moved to Tallahassee, FL in 2012 where he currently lives.

Summer Hill Seven is the former president of the Big Bend Poets & Writers based in Tallahassee, FL. He is the author of the Poemedy Trilogy, a three volume work that introduces the particulars of the poetic form known as poemedy.

Two of his haikus (included in this volume) are in the Voice of Trees Project, a public art installation, made possible in partnership with Italian artist Giovanna Iorio. The Voices of Trees Project is an effort to preserve the voices of poets and link their work to the landscape. Tallahassee and New York City, the only United States locations, join a global Voice of Trees community which includes Italy, France, England, New Zealand, Canada, Germany, Greenland, Ireland, Spain, Japan and the Netherlands.

He was the first Black president and first two-term president of the student senate at Richard Stockton University, where he graduated (honors) with a degree in political science and a certification in African-American studies in 1987. He graduated from the New York University School of Law with a Juris Doctorate. He graduated from the University of Delaware with a Masters in the Fine Arts in Acting from the Professional Theatre Training Program (PTTP). He is an alumnus of Princeton University's school of Public Policy, State University of New York, Binghamton's Graduate Theatre program and the Rand Graduate School of Public Policy.

He graduated from elementary school at Philip Schuyler Elementary School in Albany, NY and High School at the Sister Clara Muhammad School in Philadelphia, PA.

Printed in the USA
CPSIA information can be obtained
at www.ICGtesting.com
JSHW022118060124
54835JS00001B/52

9 781665 552820